ANDRE DAWSON

Books in the **Today's Heroes** Series

ANDRE DAWSON

by Andre Dawson

with Tom Bird

Property of
Northeast Christian Academy

ZondervanPublishingHouse
Grand Rapids, Michigan

A Division of HarperCollinsPublishers

Andre Dawson
Copyright © 1994 by Andre Dawson

Requests for information should be addressed to:
Zondervan Publishing House
Grand Rapids, Michigan 49530

Library of Congress Cataloging-in-Publication Data

Dawson, Andre.
Andre Dawson / by Andre Dawson with Tom Bird.
p. cm. – (Today's heroes)
Abridged from author's Hawk.
ISBN 0–310–41181–5
1. Dawson, Andre—Juvenile literature. 2. Baseball
players—United States—Biography—Juvenile literature. I.
Bird, Tom, 1956–   . II. Dawson, Andre. Hawk. III. Title.
IV. Series.
GV865.D39A3 1994b
796.357'092–dc20
[B]   94-36539
                                                                 CIP
                                                                  AC

Edited by Lori J. Walburg
Cover design by Mark Veldheer
Cover illustration by Patrick Kelley
Interior illustrations by Gloria Oostema

Printed in the United States of America

96 97 98 99/ ❖ LP /10 9 8 7 6 5 4 3

To my son, Darius, and my daughter, Amber,

my most important reasons

for deciding to retire from baseball.

—Andre Dawson

To my son, Chris,

a constant, loving reminder

of how much fun

life really can be.

—Tom Bird

Contents

Chronology of Events

1954 Andre Dawson is born July 10, 1954.

1960 Baptized in his neighborhood church.

1963 Plays his first Little League game.

1971 Severely injures knee playing high school football.

1972 Graduates from Southwest Miami Senior High; goes to Florida A & M and makes the baseball team.

1975 Drafted by Montreal Expos; goes to Lethbridge, Alberta, minor-league team.

1976 Called up by Expos in September and gets first major-league hit.

1977 Named National League Rookie of the Year.

1978 Marries Vanessa Turner.

1980 Wins first Golden Glove Award as a center fielder.

1981 Starts first All-Star game; leads Expos to within one game of World Series.

1983 Voted by peers as the Best Player in the Game.

1984 Wins first Golden Glove Award as a right fielder.

1986 Refuses the Expos' collusion-based offer.

1987 Grandmother dies; signs with the Chicago Cubs for half of what Expos were offering; becomes National League Most Valuable Player.

1989 Hits 300th career home run and logs 2000th hit; son Darius is born.

1990 Daughter Amber is born.

1992 Signs as a free agent with the Boston Red Sox.

1993 Hits his 400th career home run.

1994 Recurring knee problems convince him to retire.

Andre Dawson

1

Mamma

There is no other stadium quite like the Chicago Cubs' Wrigley Field. One of the things that makes it so special is that the fans are nearly right on top of you, especially in the outfield, where I play.

I'll never forget a voice that spoke to me out of the stands when I was playing with the Montreal Expos in 1986.

"Forget those Canadians," the voice said. "Come and play for the Cubbies. We'd love to have you."

Those words got me thinking. I knew that the soft grass of Wrigley Field would ease the pain of my achy knees. So at the end of the year when the contract talks between the Expos and me broke down, I signed with the Cubs.

With the Cubbie faithful behind me in 1987, my first year with the club, I was having the finest season of my career. Going into the final home game of the season, I was leading the National League with forty-six home runs, 137 runs batted in, and sixteen game-winning hits.

"MVP! MVP! MVP!" the fans cheered as I walked from our dugout to the on-deck circle.

During this at bat, my final one of the season at Wrigley, they wanted a home run, the final capping blow to the great season we had shared together. And I wanted to give it to them.

As I listened to them cheer for me, I could feel the muscles in my face begin to tighten into my trademark stare.

Bill Dawley was on the mound for the St. Louis Cardinals. In the past, Dawley had been very successful at striking me out on bad pitches.

However, before I stepped up to the plate that afternoon, I had already decided that I would not swing at the first two pitches, which I figured would be out of the strike zone. Then when Dawley fell behind in the count, he would be forced to throw me a hittable pitch right across the center of the plate.

Andre Dawson

Sure enough, that's exactly what happened. When he finally threw me a pitch I could hit, I was ready. The ball flew off my bat and over the left-field wall. Once again, I had delivered. The fans couldn't believe it. They were cheering so hard that I was afraid some of them might accidentally fall out of the upper deck.

At the end of the inning I went back out to my position in right field. Suddenly the greatness of that moment and the thrill of the entire season caught up with me. Tears came to my eyes. I just couldn't believe I had been so blessed. Through watery eyes, I looked up into the powder-blue sky.

"Thank you, Mamma, and thank you, Lord Jesus," I said.

Just then my grandmother's image appeared in my mind. I was maybe two or three years old, sitting with her at the table in her kitchen. The usual warm smile was on her face. I felt very loved. Looking directly into my eyes, she was speaking softly to me.

"Andre," Mamma said, "I have something very important that I want to show you, something that will change your life forever."

I looked up at her.

"Andre, do you know who God is?" she asked.

I shook my head.

"God is the maker of all things, the father of us all," she explained.

She could see the interest in my eyes.

"Do you want to talk to God, son?" she smiled. "Do you want to tell him how much you love him and how thankful you are for all that he's given you?"

I smiled in reply.

"Take your hands like this," she said, positioning my hands to pray. "Then close your eyes."

I did as she said.

"Then just open your heart and speak to God," she said.

I opened my eyes. "But how do I know that he'll hear me?" I asked.

She chuckled. "Because God hears everything and answers every prayer." She paused a moment to make sure that I understood and that I had no other questions. "Are you ready to give it a try?" she asked.

I nodded my head.

"Good, then let's pray to God together," she said, wrapping her hands around mine and closing her eyes. "Our Father, who art in heaven . . ."

Mamma was absolutely right about God. What she taught me that day would change my life forever.

Andre Dawson

2

The Proudest
Woman Alive

More than anything else, reading the Bible
and praying helped my ancestors cope with the
pain of slavery. The Bible was the only book that
the plantation owners allowed them to read. It
was also their only form of education. In my
family, reading the Bible was so important that
my great-grandfather, Edward Harrell, learned
to read by reading it to my great-great-grand-
father, who had gone blind.

In between constant droughts and boll weevil attacks, my great-grandfather did his best to scrape out a living for his family. He farmed whatever he could, from sweet potatoes to corn. He also hunted anything—rabbits, squirrels, possum—to help feed his family. Then, in 1926, he moved his family to a small black neighborhood in Miami, Florida.

In our family, every person's life is seen as a ministry. My great-grandfather soon became a deacon in the local Baptist church. He offered good advice to anyone who needed it. And he never took a drink in his life. "If you're going to be a man, be a man," I often heard him say to my uncles. "You don't have to prove anything to anybody by pouring booze inside of you."

Most of all, I remember my great-grandfather's family prayer meetings. At sunrise on Christmas and Easter, all my cousins, aunts, uncles, brothers, and sisters would meet at his house to pray.

After my great-grandfather passed away, his eldest daughter, my grandmother, Eunice Taylor, took over as the spiritual leader of our family. My grandmother and her husband bore four children, my mother, Mattie, and her three younger brothers, Curtis, John, and Theodore.

I was born when my mother was a fifteen-year-old high-school sophomore. My father,

Floyd Dawson, was a few years older. He refused to marry my mother and decided instead to join the army. Since he was never around, my uncles unselfishly filled in for him and became like fathers to me.

My grandmother was the closest person to God that I would ever meet in my life. I called her Mamma. She never had anything but praise for everything and everyone, and she caringly stepped in to raise me for my mother, who was always busy with school or her work as a baker.

Mamma became my primary role model. From her I learned what I would need to know to be a success at life. Not only did she teach me how to pray, but she introduced me to the importance of the church as well.

One Sunday, when I was six or seven years old, I went to Mamma's house early in the morning. "Andre," Mamma asked me that day, "would you like to be baptized?"

I didn't understand what she was talking about. But trusting her as I did, I nodded.

In no time at all she had me dressed in my Sunday best. She paraded me up to the front pew of the church and sat me down beside her. After a good portion of the service had passed, she led me out into the aisle, turned me over to the pastor, gently kissed me on the cheek, and whispered, "I'm very proud of you, son."

The rest happened so fast that it went by in a blur. The next thing I knew the pastor was mumbling some words and pushing me under some cold water. After the pastor had loosened his grip, I began looking around for Mamma. The expression on her face confirmed it all. My baptism had made her the proudest woman alive.

3

A Bad Decision

For as long as I can remember, I have always loved to swing a bat, a stick, or whatever I could get my hands on.

At age four, I broke off my first mop handle and scurried outside to hit some stones. At six, I sent my first rock sailing through one of the neighbor's windows. The following summer, I broke my first and only windshield.

The Lord seems to have wanted me to become a ball player, because he chose the perfect family for me. My uncles loved to play ball. They often played stickball, because it could be played in the street. But softball was their favorite game.

My uncles loved the Dodgers. After all, they were the first team to sign a black man, Jackie Robinson, into big-league baseball. And they used to play some spring exhibition games in nearby Miami Stadium. Thus the Dodgers became my favorite team as well.

I ate, slept, and dreamt about the Dodgers. I listened to every one of their games that I could, and I constantly made up mock box scores, pitting the Dodgers against this or that team. Of course, the Dodgers always won. My favorite players were Jim Gilliam, Sweet Lou Johnson (I just loved the way that the Dodger public address announcer used to say his name, *Louuuuuuuu*), and Tommie Davis.

When the Dodgers played the Yankees in the 1963 World Series, and for every fall classic that they appeared in when I was a boy, I'd skip school to stay home and watch their games on television.

Because Miami was segregated, our neighborhood didn't receive any funding to cover the cost of starting a boys' baseball league. My oldest uncle, Curtis, who was a real go-getter, didn't think that was fair. So he decided to start a little league of his own.

Andre Dawson

Uncle Curtis stirred up a lot of enthusiasm. Soon neighbors were holding fund raisers and giving donations. My mom blanched fifty pounds of peanuts at a time to be sold at the games. In no time at all Uncle Curtis was able to buy all our bats, balls, bases, gloves, helmets, caps, and T-shirts.

My first year in the league, our team went all the way up to the championship game. As usual, I arrived at the ball park early, ready for the biggest game of my life. I began to get nervous when our coach was late.

I went over and tugged on Uncle Curtis's sleeve. "Where's the coach?" I asked.

Uncle Curtis shrugged me off. "I don't know," he said.

I sat back down on the bench. But before long, my nervousness got the better of me. So I went back to Uncle Curtis, who was busily filling out our batting line-up card. "What will we do if he doesn't come?" I asked.

"You just sit and wait," he said sternly. "Do what you're told."

But not three minutes had passed before I was up and bugging Uncle Curtis again. This time, he took me by the shoulders and said, "Andre, I can't have you pestering me. You're benched for the game."

I was crushed. I slunk back to the bench and sat there through the whole game, my head low. Afterwards, I rushed home to talk to Mamma.

She listened to me carefully, and then she said, "Son, your job as a player is to play, not to coach. When you were trying to tell your uncle what to do, you were being disrespectful. Your uncle was absolutely right to bench you."

That day taught me a lesson I would never forget. I never complained to a coach or a manager again.

I performed well enough during the season to land a spot on the twelve- and thirteen-year-old all-star team. Although I mainly handled the club's score-keeping chores, I went along when we traveled to another part of Miami to play an all-white all-star team. There Uncle Curtis taught me another important lesson.

We beat the white team soundly, so they brought in older kids to play. Uncle Curtis then put in *his* older kids, who promptly whipped the white team again! No one got mad; it was all in good fun. Both teams gladly shook hands and went home happy. That's how baseball *should* be played!

I did so well playing in my uncle's baseball league that I was even more convinced that someday I would make it to the bigs. But I had

Andre Dawson

trouble convincing other people of that dream. In junior high, I wrote down on a questionnaire that I wanted to be a major-league ball player. When my counselor read my response, she smirked and said, "Okay, Andre, what do you *really* want to be?"

Even if my counselor didn't believe in me, though, *I* fully believed that I would become what God wanted me to be: a big-league baseball player.

* * *

"Listen to yourself," my grandmother once counseled me. "Weigh every decision very carefully before going forward. If you don't feel right about something, don't do it.

"Maybe you don't understand why you feel a certain way, but quite possibly God is trying to warn you about something," she continued. "If you're a Christian, that will happen to you a lot. That's just one of the ways that God takes care of us and protects us from all the traps and temptations of life."

As a seventeen-year-old junior at Southwest High School in South Miami, I discovered exactly what she meant.

I had a bad feeling about going out for the football team. But since all of my buddies had gone out, I decided to do so, too. One day during practice, one of our tight ends came across the field to block me. I was playing free safety. Trying to get out of his way, I slipped in the mud and fell. One of his spikes slipped through my face guard and ripped a large gash in my right cheek. It took eight stitches to close it back up. I still have the scar to this day.

Right after that I quit the team. I had a baseball career to protect, and I didn't want to ruin it by playing football. Eventually, however, I let one of the assistant coaches talk me into coming back to the team.

A few months later when we were playing North Miami in our fourth game of the season, I dropped back into pass coverage, and one of my teammates was blocked into me. His helmet hit my knee. I rolled back and forth in pain. I knew that I was seriously hurt, but the trainers told me that I had only strained a ligament in my knee and sent me home.

Later that night I started to get a burning sensation in my knee. The next morning my mother rushed me to the hospital. I was diagnosed as having torn cartilage and torn ligaments. I was immediately admitted to the hospital, and surgery was performed the following morning.

I was in the hospital for five days before being released with a thigh-high cast. That cast was a constant and painful reminder that I had not listened to the Lord's warning. Even after the cast was finally removed, I still had to wear a big knee brace when I played baseball.

Because of the brace, no big-league scouts cared to come around and watch me play anymore. Yet my love for the game grew stronger every day. I felt deeply that I would still play pro baseball, and I prayed that God would help me fulfill his calling for me—in spite of my bad knee.

Andre Dawson

4

Pop's Country

Even though I had been the first black ever named to the *Miami News'* All-Miami High-School Baseball Team, I didn't get drafted by a big-league club or offered a scholarship by any college or university. So I decided to follow in the footsteps of my uncles and attend Florida A & M, an all-black university in Tallahassee, Florida.

Although A & M didn't have a national reputation for greatness, sports fans in Florida recognized it. Many great athletes had attended A & M, including Olympic gold medalist sprinter and all-pro wide receiver Bob Hayes; pro basketball player Walt Bellamy; Harlem Globetrotter Tommy Mitchell; the first black to win a major tennis championship, Althea Gibson; and dozens of others.

The Rattler's baseball team was under the direction of Costa "Pop" Kittles, one of the closest men to God whom I ever had the privilege to meet. Pop saw coaching baseball as his God-given ministry to the world. What he shared with his players stayed with them long after their playing days had passed.

"No one ever left Pop's company without being moved," my uncle Theodore, whom we called Bo, once told me. Bo had played at A & M for Pop before going on to play professionally in the Pittsburgh Pirates minor-league system.

Pop made me feel at home right from the very beginning.

"We heard you may be coming out," he greeted me at the Rattler's try-out camp. "I'm glad you're here, son."

I was offered a partial scholarship after the try-out camp. Pop told me that if I made the line-up the following spring I would be awarded a full scholarship. Sure enough, I did.

I majored in physical education. In my sophomore year, for the first time in my life, I learned about weight training. Armed with

Andre Dawson

the knowledge, I began building, shaping, and strengthening my body.

By my junior year, I no longer looked anything like the scrawny kid that had stepped onto A & M's campus fighting for a scholarship. I had added plenty of muscle to support my 6'3" frame. I had also strengthened my knee enough that I no longer had to wear the cumbersome knee brace. As a result, scouts once again began turning out to watch me play.

Pop had put together a real competitive bunch of guys for my junior year. I wasn't the only star on the team. In fact, that year we swept the Hurricanes of the University of Miami in a doubleheader. They were ranked number one in the country at the time.

Later that season we traveled to Valdosta, Georgia, to play Valdosta State. Before then we had played white teams from all over the country and never had any problems. But Valdosta was a different story. The fans, the umps, and the players were all gunning for us right from the minute our bus pulled into the parking lot. A fight broke out. Things got even worse. Finally, with a riot on the verge of breaking out, the umpires stopped the game and asked us to leave, which we gladly did.

That year Pop led us to his eighth first-place

finish in the conference. Yet, because of racism, we still didn't receive an invitation to play in the NCAA tournament.

We were all hurt and disappointed. But Pop wouldn't let us end our season on that note. "Boys," he told us, "you have a lot to be proud of. I don't want any of you walking away from this season with your head down. We had a great season. We won our conference. We were the only club in the country to beat Miami, the number-one team in the nation, twice.

"No, we didn't get invited to the NCAA tournament. So what? That's just the way that things go.

"Use this moment, boys. Use this moment to reflect on what it takes to be a winner, to rise to the next level. And pray to God that things improve for each one of you, for us as a team, and for this country as a whole."

The lesson that Pop taught us remains with me to this day.

A few weeks later I was chosen by the Montreal Expos in the eleventh round of the 1975 major-league draft. After a try-out with the Expos, I was offered a $2000 signing bonus. I decided to leave college before my senior year to pursue the dream of a lifetime—playing in the big leagues.

Andre Dawson

5

Vanessa

In 1975, I was assigned to play for the Expo's Rookie League club in Lethbridge, Alberta. Lethbridge is a friendly little town nestled away in the majestic Canadian Rockies. What I remember most about Lethbridge is the long bus rides. Our nearest opponent in Montana was nine hours away!

While at Lethbridge I broke most of the records set by former big league all-star Steve Garvey. I also led the league in homers and hits and was named the Pioneer League Player of the Year.

The following season, the Expos assigned me to play in Quebec City. Quebec City was the coldest place that I had ever been in my life. Despite the weather I was determined to make it to the big leagues. As a result, I got off to a great start. I was at the top of the league in batting when two of the Expos collided in the outfield. Both had to be put on the disabled list. Minor-league stars Ellis Valentine and Gary Roenicke were called up to take their places. I was sent to Denver to fill one of the spaces vacated by Valentine and Roenicke. I was one step away from the bigs.

At Denver, I hit twelve homers in my first fourteen games. A few months later I got my own call up to the Expos. I got my first big-league hit on September 13 off future Hall of Famer Steve Carlton. As a result, the Expos invited me to spring training, where I won a starting job with the big club in 1977.

Since being granted a franchise in 1972, the Expos had been one of the worst teams in baseball. But in 1977 things were starting to look up. The club had a lot of talented young players such as Valentine, Warren Cromartie, and future all-stars Gary Carter and Larry Parrish. And they also had added a few seasoned veterans through trades and the free agent market. They acquired

Andre Dawson

Dave Cash, who had some great years with the Philadelphia Phillies; Tony Perez, who had been a major player in Cincinnati's Big Red Machine of the seventies; and steady Chris Speier, whom they got from the San Francisco Giants.

The club had also gone out and signed Dick Williams as our manager. Williams had won everywhere he had been. In Boston, he led the Red Sox to the World Series in 1967. In Oakland, he led the A's to three consecutive American League pennants from 1971–73.

Dick was a real take-charge guy who preferred to play day-in and day-out with a set lineup. So the type of players that the Expos had put together suited him just fine.

The infield was composed of Carter behind the plate, Parrish at third, Speier at shortstop, Cash at second, and Perez at first. In left field, he had Cromartie, who was also from Miami and who would eventually become one of my closest friends. I was in center field and Valentine in right. With our team, the Expos felt we would some day bring a World Series crown back to Montreal.

Though we didn't win the pennant, 1977 was a good year for the team as well as for me. The club won twenty more games than it had the previous season. I hit .282 with nineteen homers and sixty-five RBIs, stats good enough for me to be selected as the National League's Rookie of the Year.

On a personal level though, '77 was the loneliest and most painful year of my life. I was okay at the ball park. But as soon as I returned home to the four barren walls of my apartment in Montreal, I went crazy.

For the first time in my life, I put too much pressure on myself. I began having trouble breathing. I could feel my blood pressure sky-rocketing. It was horrible. I began to feel that I needed a companion, someone who would be with me always, someone whom I could take care of and who would take care of me.

Unfortunately, up until that time I hadn't been much of a ladies' man. I had only dated three women, and I was deathly shy and quiet.

After I returned home to South Miami at the end of the season, I wasn't actively looking for a wife. But if God had any strong suggestions, I was more than willing to listen.

A few months after arriving back home I received an invitation to attend the yearly opening of the Coconut Grove Dinner Theatre, a real first-class event. I didn't want to get stuck taking one of my sisters as my date. So I began asking some of my friends for suggestions on whom I

Andre Dawson

could take. The name Vanessa Turner came up almost immediately.

I had known Vanessa, who was a few years younger than I was, since the tenth grade. She used to come over to our house to have my sisters braid her hair. And she had dated one of my buddies. In fact, I may have been the reason she broke up with him! We used to kid around with each other back then, but nothing ever came of it.

I hadn't seen Vanessa for quite some time. So I made a point to drive by her parents' home, which was only a few blocks away from our house. When I rode by she was leaving the house. She was nicely dressed and looked very pretty. Finally I got the nerve to ask her to go out with me. She accepted.

Then I asked her out a second time and another time after that. It took me until the end of the second date to hold her hand. By the third date I had finally worked up enough nerve to kiss her good night.

After two months of dating her I decided that I was ready to ask her to marry me. When I brought up the subject, we spoke about it in great depth. Neither of us really knew if we were in love, but it definitely appeared that the Lord wanted us to be together.

The next day I bought her an engagement

ring. Then I made a trip over to her parents' house to ask her mother for Vanessa's hand in marriage. I was too chicken to ask her father. Vanessa had always been his little baby, and I was frightened that he would give me a hard time. To my relief, Mrs. Turner gave me her blessing.

Even though Vanessa and I were not getting married until after the '78 season, I left for spring training knowing that I would have to be alone for only one more season.

6

One Game Away

For the next few seasons, Expo team officials and owners allowed us to mature and grow
as a team. But after a third-place finish in 1978,
a second-place finish behind the Pittsburgh
Pirates in '79, and another second-place finish,
this time to Philadelphia, in 1980, they began
losing their patience with us. They wanted us to
take them to the World Series.

Dick Williams was still our manager. However, it was obvious that he was going to be fired
if we didn't win the pennant. Unfortunately, man-
agement chose the worst of all seasons to

expect Dick to do what had never been done before. In 1981, the major-league players were threatening a strike. The strike was on everyone's mind and made more headlines than the scores of our games.

No one knew what to expect as the proposed strike date rapidly approached. Expecting the worst, Dick played it smart, viewing each game as if it would be our last of the season. When the players finally went out on strike, we had a thirty to twenty-five record and were in third place behind the Phils and Cardinals.

The strike went longer than any of us anticipated it would. So when it finally ended most of us weren't in baseball-playing shape. In a stroke of genius, the club's president and general manager, John McHale, flew us all down to the team's complex in West Palm Beach, Florida, for a mini spring training. Thus when the season began again, man-for-man, we were probably in better shape than any other club.

Realizing that, McHale anticipated a quick start. When we didn't get out of the gate as quickly as he had wanted, he fired Dick and replaced him with Expo scouting director Jim Fanning.

We put together a real charge and wound up winning the division's crown for the second

Andre Dawson

half of the season. We were rewarded with the opportunity to play the Philadelphia Phillies, the first half winner, in the first round of the play-offs. Behind pitcher Steve Rogers, who got hot at the end of the season, we defeated the Phils and moved onto the next round of the play-offs. If we beat the Dodgers, who had defeated the Houston Astros in the first round, we would move on to play the American League representative in the World Series.

After splitting the first two games of the series played in Los Angeles, we then split games three and four held in Montreal. The fifth and final game pitted Ray Burris against the ace of the Dodger's staff, Fernando Valenzuela. Rogers had already started a game three days earlier and was unavailable to start. But he let Fanning know that he was willing to pitch in a relief roll if necessary.

Early on, it looked as if we were going to have our way with Fernando. In the first inning, we had runners on first and third with no one out when I settled into the batter's box. Without an RBI in any of the nine play-off games I had appeared in, I was hungry for a big hit.

I felt my fingers wrap around the bat a little tighter than usual. Finally, after working the count, I got Fernando just where I wanted him. I

40   *Andre Dawson*

fixed my gaze upon him once more. I was sure that he was going to throw me a pitch that I could hit, which he did.

Technically, there is a fine line between the hitting of a ground ball, a fly out, and a home run. Even the slightest bit of tension on the part of a batter can make a big difference.

As Fernando's pitch approached the plate, I could feel the extra tension in my body. I wanted to come through too badly. I was trying too hard. The million-dollar-a-year contract I had signed before the season was having its effect.

As the ball crossed the plate, I took my mightiest cut. The ball jumped off of my bat, rolling in the direction of Dodger shortstop Bill Russell, who quickly turned the ball into a 6–4–3 double play. The run that scored from third on the play gave us our final run of the year.

Fernando settled down immediately after that inning, and we went into the ninth inning tied one to one. Burris had pitched heroically up to that point but was out of steam. So Fanning brought in Rogers. After Rogers quickly retired the first two batters in the inning, Los Angeles centerfielder Rick Monday stepped to the plate. His solo home run off Rogers would prove to be the difference. The Dodgers were on their way to play the Yankees in the World Series. We were on our way home.

Although 1981 was easily the finest season of my pro career, I would have immediately traded my title of *Sporting News* Player of the Year, my first appearance in an All-Star game, and my second Golden Glove Award for a chance to play in the World Series.

7

Timmy

In 1982 the Lord called upon me to come to the aid of one of my very best friends.

Though we had known each other for only a few seasons, Expos outfielder Tim Raines and I were like brothers. Both of us were from Florida; Timmy was from the Orlando area. Warren Cromartie, another friend and player from Florida, called the three of us "the I-95 connection" after the interstate highway that runs north and south in Florida. And Timmy and I complemented each other well. He was talkative while I was always quiet. He was funny while I was serious. He was messy while I was extremely neat and tidy.

I'll never forget the first time that Timmy and I spoke to each other. It was during the 1980 season. After having a tremendous season in the minors, Timmy was recalled by the Expos in September. He was given the locker next to mine.

His first day with the team, I introduced myself and offered him my hand.

"You don't remember me, do you?" he asked after shaking my hand.

"Sure I do," I replied, startled. "You're Raines. I've seen you around during spring training."

"That's not what I mean," he said.

"What then?" I asked, beginning to get a bit irritated.

"Orlando, 1977."

"Orlando, 1977?" I repeated.

"Orlando, 1977," he said again. "Don't you remember? I asked for your autograph, and you told me to buzz off."

"What?" I asked with great surprise. I always made it a point to sign autographs and took a huge amount of pride in never turning anyone away.

"I was with my high school baseball team," he continued. "We had come to watch you guys

Andre Dawson

play the Twins during spring training. You were a rookie, and you just flat out refused to sign my glove."

Up to this day, Timmy still kids me about not signing his glove, and I keep denying that he ever asked me.

By 1982, Timmy was seen as one of the premier players in the Expos organization. But that year he ran into an obstacle he couldn't handle.

It all started when Timmy just didn't seem to be himself. Usually Timmy talked and joked constantly, but he grew quiet and depressed. Cro and I tried to jar him out of it, but nothing seemed to work. Finally he just stopped hanging around with us. Neither of us were terribly worried at the time. We just figured that he needed a little time and space to himself. So we let him go.

A few weeks later, Timmy failed to show up for a game. McHale called him to see if he was all right. Timmy told him that he was sick. McHale sent the team doctor over to check on him.

Once there, the doctor sensed that something wasn't right. Promising that he wouldn't go back to McHale with anything that Timmy confided in him, the physician gave Timmy a chance to come clean. Timmy told the doctor about his cocaine habit. He also gave the doctor permission to share what he had been told with McHale.

The next day McHale called Timmy into his office. Timmy told McHale that he had tried to fit in with a group of older players on the club who used cocaine. After trying it, he had gotten addicted. Finally the addiction got the better of him. When he wanted to stop using it, they wouldn't let him.

Timmy's wife, Virginia, called me the next day. She asked me to keep an eye on him. I gladly agreed. From that point forward, Timmy lived in my back pocket. Everywhere I went, he followed.

Though I was sorry for the situation that Timmy had fallen into, I was glad that he had chosen me to run to. I was proud of him for facing his situation like a man by admitting he had a problem and doing something about it. And as a result, we grew even closer. The Lord has a marvelous way of taking a bad situation and turning it to good.

Once Timmy told me that he imitated me because I was his model for what a baseball player and a man should be. Tears came to my eyes. Nothing—not even the love of the fans—

Andre Dawson

can compare to the honor of receiving love and respect from your peers.

The same month I heard about Timmy's addiction, another incident happened that changed my relationship with the Expos. One day I went shopping with Jerry White, one of our reserve outfielders and another good friend of mine. Jerry was looking for a new stroller for his baby girl. So we decided to go to a well-known department store in Montreal named Eatons.

As we walked along, three men approached us from behind. Each one had a gun. Two of the men snuck up behind Jerry and me, put their guns to our heads, and forced us, face first, against a wall.

"Don't turn around, don't say anything, and put your hands above your head," the one behind me, obviously the ringleader, ordered.

I couldn't believe this was happening. I thought that it must be some sort of joke. So, smiling, I tried to turn around.

"I said don't turn around," the man warned, pushing the barrel of his gun further into my neck. "You want to be dead?"

This was no joke.

I didn't know what was happening. I was shocked and scared. I began to panic. But I was smart enough not to do something rash. I didn't

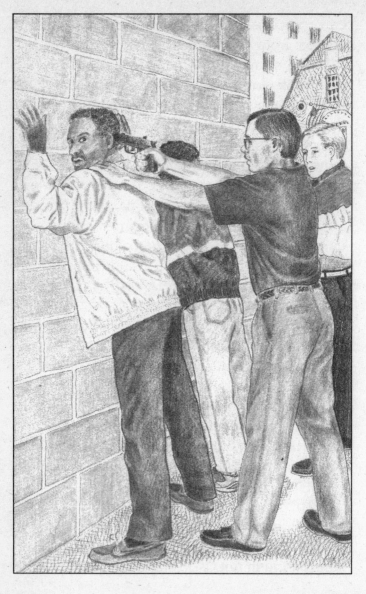

Andre Dawson

want to alarm the guys with the guns. I didn't want to do something stupid. Yet, at the same time, I wanted answers.

"What seems to be the problem?" I asked, trying to remain as calm as possible.

"I told you," the voice behind me repeated, "don't talk!"

Out of the corner of my eye I could see Jerry. He was just about to lose it.

God, I prayed, *please don't let him do anything crazy.*

The guy behind Jerry grabbed the shopping bag out of his hand and started going through it. I closed my eyes and kept praying.

When I looked up, I could see the man with his gun to Jerry's head. He was holding Jerry's wallet.

"Oh, no," the man moaned.

"What?" the guy behind me asked.

"These aren't the guys."

"What do you mean they aren't the guys?"

"Do you know who these guys are?" he responded, handing Jerry's open wallet to his partner.

Both men stepped back from Jerry and me.

"Ah, we're real sorry, gentlemen," the guy behind me said.

"I guess we made a mistake," the third one chimed in.

Their apology wasn't enough for Jerry, who grabbed his shopping bag and wallet out of their hands.

"Ah, we're real sorry," one of them said again. "But you guys fit the description of two robbery suspects."

"You mean we're black, right?" asked Jerry.

They didn't reply.

"I guess we must all look alike. Isn't that right, gentlemen?" he continued.

The men just lowered their heads and didn't respond.

"Come on," Jerry said, grabbing me by the arm. "Let's get out of here."

I was still in shock. I couldn't believe that a loaded gun had been cocked and pointed at my head for no reason. I couldn't believe that I had almost lost my life simply because I was black.

The following afternoon, Jerry and I made it a point to meet with McHale. We wanted to report what had happened to us and ask his cooperation in extracting a public apology from the police.

He listened attentively and promised to take care of the situation. We took him at his word. But nothing ever came of it. As a result I began

Andre Dawson

to see the Expos from a whole different perspective.

*   *   *

Even though I was chosen by my peers as the finest player in the game in 1983, my life was continuing to change all around me, and I wasn't sure if I was ready to change with it.

For several years now, the baseball owners had freely given out million-dollar-a-year contracts. But their overspending was beginning to catch up with them. They wanted to stop. Unable to police themselves, they began to turn to less-than-honest methods of curbing their spending habit.

Cro, who was a free agent after the '83 season, was one of the first ones affected. No team was willing to offer him the money he was worth. He could either accept unfair treatment by the big-league owners or go elsewhere. He chose to go elsewhere.

Yomiuri, Japan would be his new home. The Yomiuri Giants, Japan's Central League champs, would be his new team. His manager would be the Giant's legendary home-run king, Sahahto Oh.

Meanwhile, back at home, something was

wrong with Mamma. Worried, my mother moved Mamma in with her.

When I got home that off-season, I could see that Mamma was no longer her witty, loving self. She had become forgetful, withdrawn, depressed. Often, she would get disoriented and confused. Other times, she would shut herself inside her room for long periods and not come out.

Here I was, a twenty-seven-year-old married man, and I was scared to death of losing my grandmother. No one seemed to have any answers for her problems, including the doctors we took her to see. It was all one big mystery.

We tried to remain as positive as possible. However, she kept getting worse. After a while it became obvious that something had to be done. She had gotten to the point where she needed more help than we could give her. We had no other choice but to move her to a rest home.

When I left for spring training the next year, I kept hoping and praying that when I returned, she would be better.

Andre Dawson

8

Painful Years

I had surgery on my knees several times since sustaining my near career-ending injury in high school. But they had never really forced me to consider going on the disabled list until 1984.

That season, the pain became so severe that I was unable to get a jump on the ball in the outfield. The same was true on the base paths, where I used to be a terror. Playing in the cold, damp climate of eastern Canada on the rock-hard artificial turf of Montreal's Olympic Stadium was the worst thing possible for my knees.

At the plate, my knee would often buckle. I tried to compensate by trying different approaches to hitting. In no time at all my hands, stride, gate, and shoulders were all out of sync.

Opposing pitchers alertly picked up on my inabilities and threw me nothing but pitches they knew I couldn't handle. Early in the season, I was struggling to keep my batting average over .200.

Fans don't usually understand the extreme pain that professional athletes often endure. As a result, the fans and media of Montreal began getting down on me. Fortunately, my teammates, friends, and family members were much more aware of what I was going through.

Cro, who telephoned regularly from Japan, tried to brighten me up by making me laugh. He told me about the oddities of Japanese baseball. "Homey, you're not going to believe it," he said. "They replay tie games over here."

Timmy put in his two cents, too.

"Hey, Homey," he called to me one day on the field.

Looking down at my knees he asked, "How about a trade?"

"A trade?" I asked.

"Yeah, a trade," he replied. "I'll give you my legs if you give me your throwing arm."

Andre Dawson

Timmy had one of the weakest throwing arms in the league.

"Thanks for the offer," I joked, "but I'd rather have my bad knees than your lousy throwing arm."

No matter how much my friends, teammates, and family tried to cheer me up, nothing seemed to work. At age twenty-eight, I felt like an old man. The pain was that intense. Finally, about halfway through the season, I called Vanessa from a hotel room on the road. She listened while I spoke. Never in my life had I ever felt like I did that evening. I wanted to quit.

"Just wait, Pudgy," she said to me, referring to me by my nickname.

"What?" I asked. I couldn't believe what I was hearing.

"Just wait and see what happens," she replied. "You don't have to make any decisions now. Your world isn't going to come to an end today. Just take your time. Give your body the time it needs to heal. You've had pain before, and you've always gotten better. Just wait and give it some time. Later, if you want to retire, that's okay with me. All I want you to do is to be happy."

Just before the All-Star break, the Expos flew me to Columbus, Georgia, to see a physician by the name of Dr. James Andrews. Dr. Andrews specialized in problems of my nature. What he had to offer me was a mixture of both good and bad.

On the bad side, the source of my pain was a half-inch bone chip floating around in my knee. The good news was that I could continue to play without fear of further damage as long as I could somehow stomach the pain. With that in mind, I went on a hot streak as soon as I rejoined the club. I finished the season on a high note.

As soon as the following season came to an end, Vanessa and I drove up to see Mamma. I hurried into her room at the rest home, excited to see her. I wanted to give her a big hug and kiss.

She jumped back in her chair when she saw me. I was scared and confused by her reaction. I didn't know what to do. She no longer knew who I was. My heart nearly broke in two.

The doctors explained to us that she had Alzheimer's disease. Alzheimer's is a disease that attacks the mind and the body of some older people. In its later stages, it destroys the memory, the ability to speak, and the ability to move.

No one knows what causes Alzheimer's Disease. There is also no known cure.

9

Contacting the Cubs

Nineteen eighty-six was just as full of change as 1984. That year a major event would take place that would disprove much of what I believed in.

Like so many other great players, I thought that I would be with only one big-league team my entire career. I had felt that way since I was a kid. I thought, of course, that team would be the Montreal Expos.

But in 1986 the big-league owners introduced an element into the great game that would change all that. That element was called collusion. By definition collusion is a secret agreement that two or more parties make to deliberately harm another party. The owners plotted to use collusion to stop the rising salaries of players.

They planned to do this by deliberately not offering free agents the type of money they had been getting the past few years. In that way, free agents would be forced to sign on again with their original teams for whatever that team chose to offer.

Dick Moss, my agent and one of the best in the business, was the first to uncover the owners' collusion. When he shopped around Jack Morris, one of the finest pitchers in the game at the time, he got no decent offers. So Dick made his findings public: No one is willing to pay Jack Morris or anyone like him what he is worth, *because the owners had agreed not to do so.* Not only did this collusion hurt the players, but it was also against the law.

I was a free agent after the 1986 season, a time in which I had planned to receive a large amount of money that would make my family financially secure for the rest of my life. However, that was not to be the case.

Andre Dawson

Even though I had played faithfully through injuries, batting slumps, and numerous managerial changes, even though I never complained, and even though I was the club's all-time leader in just about every offensive category, the Expos offered me less money to sign with them than I had been making, and less than players for other teams were making. As much as Dick Moss and I tried to negotiate with them, they still refused to budge.

The fact that they refused me hit me hard. "Vanessa," I said to my wife one day, "I might be like Cro. I might just end up playing in Japan."

"Where?" she asked.

"Japan," I responded.

"Japan," she repeated. "Pudgy, are you crazy? You want to play in Japan?"

"Cro says it's nice over there," I said, "and they're paying him big money to play."

"Pudgy, you're crazy," she said.

I decided to drop the matter for a while. However, in my mind Japan was a real consideration.

When we didn't bite on the team's offer, the Expos tried to trade me to another big-league club. That hurt me, too. I couldn't understand why they would rather trade me than pay me. But I played along as best I could through the remainder of the season. About the only pleasant memories I have of the season were our trips into Wrigley Field. I loved to play there.

I'll never forget the voice that spoke to me out of the stands in our last visit into Wrigley of the season. "Forget those Canadians," the fan had said. "Come and play for the Cubbies. We'd love to have you."

His words touched me at a time when I was really feeling down.

The negotiations with the Expos came to a conclusion during the last home stand of the season. At Dick's request, the Expos' owner, Charles Bronfman, and some of the team's top executives made time to meet with us after a game.

After a long speech, they made their pitch: a $400,000 cut in pay spread over two years.

"A cut in pay?" I kept asking myself. "For what? What have I done to deserve a cut in pay? Play hard? Show up every day on time? Lead the team in every offensive category in the history of the club? Be a good leader? Be selected for the All-Star team? Play hurt? Win Golden Gloves? Finish second in the Most Valuable Player voting twice?"

Dick tried hard to open their eyes to how

unfair they were being, but the Expos refused to give us a reasonable offer.

As we left the meeting, Bronfman and his chief executives all had smug looks on their faces. Because of the collusion, they felt as if it would only be a matter of time before we came crawling back, begging to accept their offer.

Instead, Dick began to look for a new team for me. He knew that I was familiar with and comfortable in the National League. Thus he knew that I would prefer to stay there rather than go over to the American League. From our conversations, he also realized that I had a deep respect for the Chicago fans. In addition, he knew how I loved to play on the soft grass of Wrigley Field. So he contacted the general manager of the Cubs, Dallas Green, to arrange a meeting.

Knowing that because of the collusion Green would be unable to meet with him officially, Dick arranged a secret rendezvous with Dallas at a hotel in Chicago.

Dick knew that Green would be biting at the bit to land a player of my caliber, so he made his point quickly, telling Dallas that I was indeed available and for a price that the Cubs would definitely be able to afford.

To protect himself, Green gave Dick the

agreed-upon company lie. He told Dick that he didn't know if the team would be interested in signing me because the club already had enough outfielders. However, he let it be known, in ways that only old friends such as they would know, that he was very interested. Dick called me shortly afterwards to make arrangements with Vanessa and me to discuss my situation.

When Dick arrived in Miami a few weeks later, he didn't mention anything about his meeting with Green. However, I could sense that he was optimistic.

Dick took a considerable amount of time going over my options with me. He painted a very clear picture of what we were up against. It wasn't that the clubs didn't want me. To the contrary, they were dying to land me. Because of the collusion, they just couldn't say so, or for that matter, do much about it.

Dick cautioned me about being too optimistic. We would have to overcome a lot of hurdles for me to be able to land a position with the Cubs. According to Dick, we would probably have to somehow embarrass the Cubs into making us an offer.

Of course, we would be risking a lot in trying to do so. Two very embarrassing situations loomed as strong possibilities. First, the Cubs

Andre Dawson

could hold tightly to their collusionary company line and not respond with any offer at all. Thus I would be left with only two alternatives: to go crawling back to the Expos or to voluntarily sit out the 1987 season.

Second, they could make us an offer so low that I would be given only a fraction of what I was used to being paid. But as I saw it, we had no other alternative but to try.

I gave Dick permission to go ahead with his plan.

10

The Toughest Thing I Ever Did

Mamma's doctor telephoned right after the start of the new year. He had called to request a meeting with us as soon as possible.

Once we arrived at his office, he explained how Mamma's condition had substantially worsened. She had lost her appetite and had stopped eating completely. He had to switch her to intravenous feedings. As a result, some of her organs were beginning to shut down.

He made it very clear to us that he could

Andre Dawson

keep giving her the intravenous feedings for as long as her veins held up, which he predicted would be for no longer than a year. Or, if we decided to take her off the intravenous feedings and allow her to die in a more dignified fashion, she could last as long as two weeks.

As a family, we felt that she would prefer being taken off the intravenous feedings. That way we could take her home to die. Calling ahead, we had a hospital bed delivered to my mom's house. It was waiting for us when we arrived.

Once home, one of us was with her all of the time. We took turns sitting with her, bathing her, and feeding her. The most she could eat was Jell-O.

Each day I watched her slip away more and more. In the beginning, she had tried desperately to speak. Eventually, she was unable to say anything at all.

She went on to lose sight in one eye, and she was beginning to lose the sight in the other. Her slow, painful passing was hard on all of us. I could see the pain, stress, and tension in the faces of everyone in our family.

On the eleventh day after returning home, she curled up into a fetal position. By that time I had enough. I had seen her suffer too much.

Hiding myself away in one of the back bedrooms of my mom's house, I cried and cried.

After what seemed an eternity, I suddenly knew what I had to do. I got down on my knees and prayed to God. Never had I prayed so hard and never had I wanted an answer so quickly.

"Lord," I prayed, "Mamma would probably be better off with you. And as much as I don't want to let her go, I wish you would come and take her so that all of her suffering would finally come to an end."

It was almost as if Mamma and God were waiting for me to let her go. For the very next morning we got a call. She was dying. Vanessa and I rushed over to my mom's house. But by the time we got there, she had already passed away.

At that moment, I felt lonelier than I had ever felt before in my life.

The day of Mamma's funeral was a day that I had been dreading for years. Just knowing that I would have to say my final good-byes to her made it hard for me to get out of bed.

Vanessa was holding on securely to my arm, but I was trembling as I walked down our sidewalk to the limousine that awaited us.

At the church where Mamma's wake was being held, I was greeted by Barbara Bain, who asked me to perform a service in behalf of my family.

"Andre," she said, "your family wants to know if you would do them the honor of closing your grandmother's casket after the service?"

My heart fell to my feet. Could I do it?

I looked up. John and Curtis, my uncles, were there. So was my mom. As they awaited my reply, Vanessa squeezed my arm a little tighter, as if encouraging me to accept their request. Our eyes met. I knew that they were doing this for me. I felt strength and power entering my body. I nodded my answer.

I had been to many church services in my lifetime. Mamma had seen to that. But her memorial service seemed to be the quickest I had ever attended.

When the time arrived for me to complete my end of the service, I rose to my feet and slowly made my way to her casket. I looked down at her lying there. I knew that she would have wanted me to do this for her. But that didn't make it any easier.

I knew that I didn't have the strength to close her casket on my own. I took one long, last look at her before closing my eyes.

Dear God, I prayed silently, *please take very*

Andre Dawson

good care of her. Please keep her safe and warm and always love her.

"Thank you, Jesus," I said to myself as I suddenly found the strength to close, for the last time, the book of her life on this earth.

11

My Place in Big-League History

The day that the Lord had chosen for me to contribute to the course of baseball history came shortly after Mamma's death. Since no club had given us a substantial contract offer yet, Dick felt that it would be best to pay Dallas Green a visit at the Cubs' spring training in Arizona.

Interestingly, when we arrived at the Cubs' complex, Green supposedly was meeting secretly with other baseball officials on the progress of their collusion. When he arrived back in town that afternoon, Green was furious to see Dick and me strolling around the complex. He immediately called us into his office. All of the actions we had taken were part of Dick's plan, which was to make the Cubs an offer that they couldn't refuse and then embarrass them into accepting it.

Once Green had cooled down, Dick reached into his briefcase and pulled out a contract. With Green watching in wonder, Dick handed him the contract. Green very quickly looked it over and immediately noticed that the dollar amount that I was to be paid had been left blank. "Is this some sort of joke?" he asked.

"This is no joke, Dallas," Dick said. "Andre wants to play for the Cubs, and he will do so for any salary that is fair."

Green shook his head in disbelief. Although ball clubs have often forced contracts on ball players, never before had a player taken the reverse position with a club.

"That's why we left that section of the contract blank," Dick continued. "Feel free to fill in whatever numbers you feel are appropriate. And I guarantee you, if the numbers are fair, we will accept them."

"All that we ask," he said, "is that you get back to us within twenty-four hours. If we cannot work out a deal by that time, we will begin giving other clubs the same opportunity."

It's difficult for me to describe the sense of elation that I experienced upon leaving Green's office that day. Whether the Cubs bit on our offer or not, I had taken back control of my own life, my own destiny. That's what was most important to me.

Throughout the entire ordeal, I could feel Mamma's presence right there beside me. I knew that she had played a big part in helping me come to my decision. I also knew that she was very, very proud of me for what I was doing.

Since Dick had made it a point to make sure that the media saw us visiting Green at the Cubs' complex, it didn't take long before the news was out. Overnight, Chicago fans were buzzing about the possibility of adding me to their club. Dick wanted the added pressure from the fans to force Green's hand, which is exactly what it did.

The next day Dick called me to let me know that Green would be contacting me that afternoon. The Cubs were going to be making me an offer.

When the call finally came, Green seemed unusually nervous. Thus I expected the worst.

Maybe our plan had backfired, and he was going to come through with an insulting offer.

"Andre," he began, "we have gone over your situation in great detail, and we would like to make you an offer.

"Please be aware though," he stressed, "that the offer I am about to make is the best that we can do."

"Oh, no," I said to myself as I held my breath.

He continued, "The contract we are willing to offer you is for a guaranteed $500,000 salary for the 1987 season, plus a $150,000 bonus if you don't end up on the disabled list before the All-Star break and another $50,000 if you make the All-Star team."

I thought about his offer. The total package was for $700,000, or about half of what I had made with the Expos the previous season. My alternatives were to accept the Cubs' offer, to limp back to the Expos with my tail between my legs, or to forget about playing baseball that season. What the owners were doing wasn't fair. But it was something that I had to accept and deal with. Besides, Dick felt certain that I would be able to recoup any money I had lost from their collusion through a lawsuit that the MLPA was planning against the owners.

"Okay, Mr. Green," I said after a few seconds, "we have a deal."

Maybe I was being idealistic, but I expected Green to get excited. Instead, there was absolute silence on his end of the line before he finally spoke.

"Okay, Andre," he replied hesitantly, as if he hadn't expected me to accept his offer. "I'm, um, well, going to have to check with our attorney and then get back to you."

Of course, I knew what that meant. He had to run my acceptance by the officials he had probably been meeting with the previous day.

The half an hour that I waited for him to call back was the longest of my life. All types of thoughts ran through my mind during that time. Would he back out? What would I do if the Cubs reneged on their offer and I had to go back to the Expos? Could I live with myself if I sat out the 1987 season?

I did a lot of praying during that time as well. I prayed to Jesus for guidance and asked him to take care of me and my family, to give us direction, and to make sure that we were always following his will. I knew that he and Mamma would take care of me. They always had.

"Your will be done," I just kept praying over

and over again. "Your will be done. Your will be done."

Then the phone rang. It was Green. And this time he sounded happy.

"Andre," he said.

"Yes?" I replied.

"We have a deal," he said. "Welcome aboard. You're a Chicago Cub."

12

The Pledge

Leaving Montreal, where the fans were quiet and knew little about baseball, and going to Chicago, a city with the most knowledgeable baseball fans in the world, was like dying and going to heaven.

The day after my signing, the ticket window at Wrigley Field was overrun with excited fans.

The Cubbie players were just as excited. When I entered the Cubs' clubhouse for the first time, they all rose to their feet and gave me a standing ovation.

"I think he'll make us a contender," said Cub

Andre Dawson

second baseman Manny Trillo. I had once played with him in Montreal.

"He's quiet, but he's a real team leader," he continued. "We're all excited about getting a player like that."

The excitement was contagious.

"I jumped in the air when I heard it," added left-handed pitcher Steve Trout. "I'll have to give Dallas a big hug when I see him."

Even the younger outfielders like Thad Bosley, whose playing time would probably be limited by my presence, were happy that I had joined the team.

"If they play me, I know I can play," admitted Bosley. "But if they want me to sit on the bench and let Dawson play every day, I don't have any problem with that. The most important thing is to win. Everybody will be happy, and everybody will benefit."

Dave Martinez found himself in the same position as Bosley.

"To me it means the team has picked up a great player," he said. "All the rest of us have to do is worry about going hard every day. I don't think this will discourage anyone."

Even the media was excited. Reporters were running all over the clubhouse, getting reactions to my signing.

Possibly no one was happier about my joining the club than our manager, Gene Michael.

"He can hit third, fourth, or fifth," I overheard him saying about me. "He's one of those kind of guys."

Although Dallas told me to take my time settling in with the team, I was too anxious to hold back. So I decided to jump right in.

The next morning, I was still buzzing from the reception I had received. I needed a little time to myself just to let it all sink in. So I drove out to the Cubs' complex. While there, I took a walk out onto the baseball diamond.

I thought about all that had happened. I pondered my life, and all that I had gone through that had brought me to that moment.

I thought about Mamma, and I cried a bit. I thought about how she had brought me to Jesus. I thought about the influence that her actions had on my life. And at that moment, I decided to make a rare emotional decision.

Up until that time in my career, I had always taken a very businesslike approach to the game. I had set tangible goals for myself each season. I had set goals on how many home runs I would try to hit that season, how many bases I would try to steal, and so on. Never before had I allowed my heart, my emotions, to rule.

Andre Dawson

However, on that morning I decided not to worry about how many homers I would hit or how many bases I would steal. I decided to dedicate my efforts that season to the love and respect I had for Mamma.

That decision, as I discovered later, would make all the difference in the world.

13

Most Valuable Player

For me 1987 would become the season I had always dreamt of having.

My hot streak started in mid-April while we were in St. Louis playing the Cardinals. At the beginning of the season, I had been over-whelmed by the Cubbie fans' continued adoration and support. As a result, I had been trying too hard to please them. As often happens to a big leaguer in such a situation, I slipped into a miserable slump. However, in St. Louis that all came to an end when I broke out of a zero-for-ten streak with a game-winning grand slam.

Then it was on to Montreal, where the fans booed me. That hurt. But not as bad as my two homers, two doubles, and six runs scored hurt their Expos. I was on a roll.

The following weekend in Chicago, I had a chance to become the first Cubbie to hit the cycle—a single, double, triple, and home run in one game—since Ivan DeJesus did it in 1980. Going into my last at bat of the day, I had already hit two singles, one double, and a homer. All that stood between me and the cycle was the hardest hit of all to acquire, the elusive triple.

The fans at Wrigley, as was becoming a tradition, were all on their feet as I stepped to the plate with two outs in the ninth inning. All of them wanted to see me hit a three bagger.

Frank DePino, one of our left-handed relievers who was also a good friend, winked at me on the way out of the dugout. "I know you," he said. "You're going to hit a flare to right and dig for three."

Mike LaCoss, a real competitor, was pitching for the Giants. He got two quick strikes on me. Yet the Cubbie faithful never lost faith. They just cheered louder and louder. There was no way that I was going to let them down.

LaCoss's next pitch was the one that I had been waiting for. I did just as Frank said I would. I hit a bloop fly down the right-field line and never even thought of stopping at second. The place went wild as I slid safely into third base.

Going into our July series against the Padres at Wrigley, I had become a marked man. In fact, I'd already hit six homers off the San Diego pitching staff that season. Padres manager Larry Bowa was quoted in the newspaper as saying that his pitching staff would have to do a better job of backing me off the plate. I knew what that meant. Bowa was going to have his pitchers throw at me.

Right-hander Eric Show, a sinker ball/fastball specialist, was the ace of their staff. Someone had to set an example for the rest of the Padre pitching staff. Bowa had chosen Show to be that man.

Up until '87, Show had handled me pretty well. Going into '87 I was hitting only .091 lifetime against him. However, in our most recent trip to San Diego I had homered off him early on and then knocked him out of the game with a base hit in my very next at bat.

On July 7, I continued my streak against

him by taking him for a home run in my first at bat against him. During my second at bat of the game, he decided he'd had enough.

It all happened so fast. One second I was standing in the batter's box waiting for him to deliver his first pitch. The next thing I knew, I was lying facedown in the dirt, my head throbbing.

Only half conscious, I wasn't aware of what was going on in the field. One of our pitchers, Rick Sutcliffe, one of the biggest and toughest guys in the league, had charged Show on the mound. The only thing that kept Sutcliffe from blindsiding Show, who was caught totally unaware, were the quick reactions of Padre first baseman John Kruk, who grabbed Rick and wrestled him to the ground.

While all of this was going on I could hear our young first baseman, Leon "Bull" Durham, speaking to one of my teammates. "It's a shame we're going through this at all," he said. "We're supposed to be out here enjoying the game. But look at this guy's face."

He meant my face. For the first time I realized how badly I had been hurt. In seconds I was on my feet. I had only one goal in mind: to get Show.

I charged through the horde of Padres surounding Show, and I got so close to him that I

Andre Dawson

could see the fear in his eyes. Rick, Leon, and our first-base coach John Vukovich lunged at him as well.

With us in hot pursuit, umpire Charlie Williams grabbed Show by the arm and hurried him over to the Padre dugout. I continued to pursue with every bit of strength that I could muster. In the end, Show narrowly escaped my grasp as he scampered down the dugout stairs to the San Diego clubhouse.

The battle on the field continued long after Rick and I were ejected from the game and after I was rushed to Northwestern Hospital. Twenty-one-year-old pitching phenom Greg Maddux and manager Gene Michael were ejected in the fourth inning for drilling the Padre's catcher, Benito Santiago. Trillo was ejected shortly after. Right-hander Scott Sanderson and interim manager Johnny Oates were the last to go, thrown out when Sanderson threw at Padre Chris Brown in the eighth inning.

Tony Gywnn of the Padres, one of the finest hitters in the league, commented after the game, "Today was the first time in my life that I've been scared to go to the plate."

My injury from Show's beaning was so severe that a plastic surgeon had to be called in. It took twenty stitches to close the wound. The surgeon did a good job of pulling the scar down into the area of my mustache so it wouldn't be so visible.

To clear his name, Show wrote me a personal apology. He claimed that he had not intended to hit me with his pitch. But I knew better, so I chose not to honor his letter with a response. I can forgive, but I find it difficult to forget.

There was no way that I was going to let the injury deter me from playing in the All-Star game. I hadn't been voted onto the team in over three years, and in '87 I had been the third leading vote-getter.

By August 1, it was so hot in our game against the Phils at Wrigley that I didn't think that I would have the strength to play into the fifth inning. But since I had already hit two home runs that day, I decided to give it a try.

I struggled just to get out of the dugout and into the batter's box for my fourth at bat of the day. I thought to myself, how am I ever going to hit a home run feeling like this? But the Lord and Mamma were definitely with me that day, as they had always been. With the Cubbie faithful rooting me on, the ball just seemed to jump off of my bat and over the fence for my third dinger of the afternoon.

Andre Dawson

Miracles do happen. All you have to do is believe.

For me, there couldn't have been a truer testimony to that fact than 1987. Not only did I have the finest season of my career, but I was also named as the National League's Most Valuable Player, the first player on a last-place team ever chosen to receive the honor

14

Our Two Miracles

Nineteen eighty-eight and 1989 were the finest years of my life. Not only did I produce well both years, but, most importantly, baseball and life became fun again.

Even though Dallas Green resigned as the Cubs' general manager at the conclusion of the '87 season, the team hired very capable Jim Frey to take his place. With Frey, they also brought in Don Zimmer to serve as our manager.

Frey and Zimmer were not only real baseball people but best friends. Having both grown up together on the sandlots of Cincinnati, they were used to each other. Under the duo, the Cubs became contenders almost overnight.

In '88, Frey, who had previously served as the Cubs' farm director, moved some of the young phenoms he had been raising in the minor leagues onto the team. The new blood mixed well with the experience of the veterans. That year we improved substantially over the previous season, moving up three spots to fourth place in the division.

After the conclusion of that season, I got some miraculous news on the personal level as well. For the last seven or eight years Vanessa and I had been trying, without any success, to have a baby. By '88 we were frustrated.

Then she caught wind of a doctor with a high success rate of helping couples such as us. His name was Dr. LeMaire, and he worked out of the University of Miami's Jackson Memorial Center. Dr. LeMaire was the type of take-charge person that I like.

He suggested a procedure for us to try. And we didn't have to wait long for the results. Soon after our treatment, Dr. LeMaire's office called and left a message on our answering machine that Vanessa was pregnant! Vanessa was so happy that she started to cry.

We still have the tape. Even now when we play it we find it hard to hold back the tears.

*   *   *

The following year everything jelled for us as a team. The young kids stepped forward and turned in outstanding seasons. Youngsters Greg Maddux and Mike Bielecki were our top two pitchers, and first baseman Mark Grace, second baseman Ryne Sandberg, and Dwight Smith led us at the plate. We ended up winning the division by six games over the favored New York Mets.

Regardless of the fact that we lost four of the five games in the National League Championship Series to the red-hot San Francisco Giants, we had a lot to be proud of.

But despite all that was happening for us on the diamond, what I will remember most about 1989 happened off the field. For on August 12th our first child was born.

Like most husbands, I tried to remain calm, cool, and collected. But I was such a mess by the time we arrived at the hospital that I pulled the surgical scrubs they had for me over my clothes. By that time, I was sweating so badly that I perspired clear through both layers of clothes.

Andre Dawson

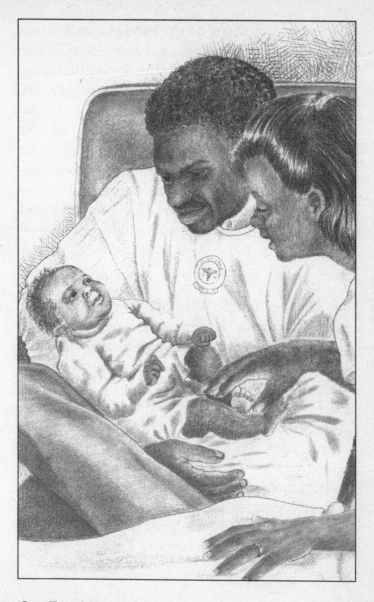

Our Two Miracles

After our son's birth, Vanessa and I took some time before deciding to name him Darius DeAndre, after the King Darius in the Bible.

In the winter of 1989, Vanessa began getting tired and sick to her stomach on a regular basis. Worried that she was seriously ill, she avoided seeing a doctor about her condition for over two months. Finally she made an appointment with a physician. Upon examining her, he discovered that the source of her problems was that she was pregnant again. We were overwhelmed with joy.

*　　*　　*

On the field, it was our pitching that fell apart during the '90 season, accounting for our demise. But even though we were way out of the pennant race by September, life was still looking really good.

On the field, I wound up hitting a career high .310, ninth in the league, with twenty-seven homers and 100 RBIs. I also finished fifth in the league with a slugging percentage of .535, tenth in extra base hits, and tied for a major-league high of twenty-one intentional bases on balls.

Off the field, my daughter Amber Channelle, our miracle baby, was born on September 5.

15

The Beginning
of the End

Big-league owners view the game of base-ball much differently than you and I. To them, it's a business. Period. How many fans a team draws to their games determines how much money an owner makes. Winning puts more fans in the seats than anything else. So winning is an owner's primary purpose.

On the other hand, if a team doesn't win then the fans don't show up. If the fans are no longer coming out to see their team play then the owners lose money. Before the owners lose too much money they usually try to blame their team's poor play on someone. Then they fire that person. Usually that person is the club's general manager or manager, or sometimes both.

That's the situation which Frey and Zimmer found themselves in entering the 1991 season. Even though the club had won the National League East Pennant in 1989 and missed going to the World Series only by a few games, in 1990 the club had not fared well. The Tribune Company began to lose money. Something had to be done.

My teammates and I were aware that Zim and Frey were on the hot seat, but we weren't aware of the behind-the-scenes actions that were being engineered to get them both fired. In fact, it didn't appear as if Zim or Frey were aware that anything was going on, either. They were just too busy trying to put together a winning team to have time to worry about anything else.

None of us went into '91 knowing what disaster awaited us at the end of the season. We were only concerned with bringing another pennant back to Chicago and with saving Zim and Frey's jobs.

Though Frey had brought in a few new top-notch players during the off-season, we didn't look much different than the Cubs that finished in fourth place the previous season. After only thirty-seven games into the season, someone had to be fired. Zim was the logical choice.

Almost overnight Zim went from being considered as the finest field general in the game in '89, when he was named as the Manager of the Year by the Baseball Writer's Association of America, the *Sporting News,* and United Press International, to being fired. Frey was forced to keep his mouth shut just to hold onto his own job.

Non-confrontational Jim Essian, a former journeyman big-league catcher, was hired to take over. After we finished the season with a losing record under Essian, it was obvious to us all that not only would Essian not be brought back, but Frey would probably be fired, too.

By the end of the season when the Cubs' Chairman Stan Cook fired Frey, a replacement didn't even have to be sought. Cook supposedly had had a replacement in mind for over eighteen months.

Larry Himes was the man he chose to take over Frey's position. Himes, who was hired by Cook apparently without even an interview or being asked for a reference, which is very rare, had been rumored to be working behind the scenes to get Frey and Zim fired since he, himself, had been let go by our cross-town rivals, the Chicago White Sox.

Before his time at the White Sox, Himes had been working in the minor leagues as a coach or a scout. In the minor leagues most of the players are only eighteen or nineteen years old, so Himes learned to treat his players like they were children needing supervision. Even when he got to the major leagues, he treated the much older and more mature White Sox players like they were kids.

For example, Himes made his players follow the rules in a twenty-five page booklet he called his *Code of Conduct*. The booklet laid out in great detail how each of his players were expected to act, speak, and dress.

One of Himes's biggest concerns was that all White Sox players wear socks. Sometimes he even snuck up behind a player and reached under the big leaguer's pant legs to see if he had socks on!

Insulted that Himes would treat them like kids, the White Sox players revolted. However, the more they refused to follow Himes's rules, the stricter he seemed to get.

Andre Dawson

Despite his reputation, I had absolutely nothing against Himes when he joined the Cubs. As far as I was concerned he had never done anything wrong to me, so why should I dislike him? All that I cared about was remaining a Chicago Cub for the rest of my career, which I felt would be a given based upon how I had done for the team since having joined them.

But when Himes tried desperately to sign Bobby Bonilla, a big-name free agent from the Pittsburgh Pirates who played the same position as me, to a long-term contract, I began to get nervous. So I asked Dick to contact Himes to see if we could work out a two-year deal, which I felt would carry through to the end of my big-league career.

Himes stated that he was indeed interested in extending my contract for a few more seasons. However, he said that he had been extremely busy since joining the club and asked if we could sit down and discuss the matter at a later date. He seemed to be very open and upfront about his situation, so we took him at his word. But when five months passed and he was still refusing to meet with us, we began to feel that he was deliberately putting us off.

Finally, with the press and fans hounding him about my signing, Himes eventually came through with an insulting offer: a big cut in pay. We rejected the ridiculous offer. And shortly after that, I had my first run-in with Himes.

During the off-season when I'm lounging around the house with my family, you can usually find me in a tee-shirt, a pair of jeans, shorts or sweats. However, during the baseball season, when I am representing a major-league team, I take a tremendous amount of pride in how I dress.

Going into the 1992 season, I had a tailor personally design some collarless suit jackets for me. I could wear them with turtlenecks during the first few weeks of the season when it was really cold. The jackets were expensive, but in wearing them, I still would be violating a rule about wearing ties listed in Himes's *Code of Conduct*.

I just about went crazy when Himes yelled at me for not wearing a tie. Here I was in a tailor-made suit jacket being reprimanded for not wearing a necktie while other guys on the club were making a joke of the entire situation! Most could be found in jeans, cowboy boots, and flannel shirts, on top of which they would wear a scraggly old tie.

I didn't want to confront Himes about the situation directly. It wouldn't have been right to

Andre Dawson

go over our manager's head. So I went to see our manager, Jim Lefebvre, about the whole situation. He listened to all that I had to say and was very understanding and sympathetic. After hearing what I had to say, he promised to talk to Himes. True to his word, a few days later Lefebvre got back to me. He had worked everything out with Himes. It was now okay for me to wear the specially made suitcoats.

Right then and there Himes stopped talking to me. He had never said much to me before then, but at least he had taken the time to say "hi" every once in awhile. But after the suit coat caper, he refused to even look at me. In fact, on one occasion he entered our clubhouse looking for someone or something. Barry Rozner, a reporter with the *Daily Herald*, and I were the only ones around. Faced with the decision of either speaking to Rozner, whom he hated, or me, Himes chose to speak to Barry.

The entire situation got so absurd that even my teammates began to notice how Himes deliberately ignored me. Though my teammates continually made jokes about the situation and I laughed along with them, Himes's mistreatment really took its toll. I just wasn't used to being hated.

By the second week of the season, my

teammates got a firsthand taste of what I had been experiencing. Himes's controlling ways began to take a hold of us all. All of us began to feel as if we were constantly being watched or spied upon.

I began to wonder if I should walk away from the game right then and there. Dealing with Himes had taken all of the fun out of playing the game.

My left knee, the one I had hurt while playing football, was bothering me as well, and I just didn't have the patience to endure the pain anymore. The club's orthopedic surgeon confirmed my worst suspicions when he told me that my knees were the worst ones that he'd ever seen.

It's amazing what a man like Himes can do to your soul. Mamma had told me how to handle devils. But she had never taught me how to deal with anyone as difficult as Himes.

Fight as I did, Himes finally got to me. By August, I just couldn't take all of the hatred anymore, and I fell into a rare batting slump. Himes, who apparently wanted to get rid of me, used the opportunity to try and prove to the Cubs that I couldn't play anymore.

While others were innocently following Himes's lead and calling for my retirernent,

Andre Dawson

Lefebvre bravely stepped to the forefront. "He's still got a lot left," he said publicly. "I guarantee it."

His words were like a message from heaven. They were just the boost of confidence and reassurance that I needed. From that point forward, I went on a five-week hitting rampage that turned my critics, with the exception of Himes, back into fans.

But no matter what I was able to accomplish, Himes seemed determined to get rid of me.

Near the end of the season, Himes called a meeting to discuss the potential make-up of the club for the next season. The coaches at that meeting couldn't believe what they were hearing. Himes, preferring to consider players from other teams instead, never once mentioned keeping me on the club.

A few weeks later, before our final game of the season at Wrigley, I attended our regular Sunday chapel service in the clubhouse. Not sure if I would see them any more, I took the time to thank all of my teammates for their support and friendship through the season. I also reminded them to keep their hearts and souls focused on their Lord Jesus Christ and that he would guide them through all their trials and tribulations for the remainder of their days.

Later that afternoon I stepped up to the

plate for my final at bat of the season at Wrigley. The loyal 23,000 Cub fans in attendance that day rose to their feet to greet me. Tears came to my eyes. I didn't want my time as a Cubbie to come to an end.

Andre Dawson

16

When the Lord Closes a Door

I wasn't the only big-name Cubbie poten-
tially becoming a free agent after the '92 season.
Both Ryne "Ryno" Sandberg, our all-star second
baseman, and Greg "Maddog" Maddux, who
most considered the top pitcher in the league,
found themselves in the same dilemma as I.

All three of us wanted to stay with the Cubs,
but only Ryno was signed. In a move that sent
shock waves throughout all of professional

sports, Himes signed him to a record-setting 7.5 million dollar a year contract.

In Himes's eyes Maddog and I were much different players than Ryno. While Ryno kept quiet on just about everything, Maddog and I spoke up in the face of injustice. We were just the type of guys that Himes despised.

But in both of our cases Himes had to protect himself. Had he let it be known that he personally did not want to sign either of us, the Cubbie fans would have lynched him. So he tried to make it look as if it was our fault that we hadn't re-signed with the Cubs.

The beginning of the end came for me on November 1 when a newspaper story, quoting reliable but unnamed sources, surfaced claiming that I would be resigned by the Cubs as early as within ten days. It was stated that the deal would keep me in a Cubbie uniform for not only the next two years, which I was seeking, but for several seasons beyond that as an announcer, coach, player, or whatever as well.

Since this was the first time that either my agent or I had heard of any such offer, Dick contacted Dennis Homerin, who was handling the negotiations for Himes. Homerin hadn't been informed of any such offer either. Dick and I both wondered if Himes had somehow started the rumor to temporarily take the heat off his back about re-signing me.

Over and over again the media kept reporting that the Cubs still wanted me. Where they were getting their information, I don't know. But Himes had refused to even speak to us about a contract since before spring training.

On the 5th of November, I filed for free agency, which the media took as a positive sign, saying that my filing actually gave me a better chance of remaining a Cub. A few weeks later, the expansion draft was conducted to fill the rosters of the Florida Marlins and the Colorado Rockies.

The media just kept reporting that it was only a matter of time before the Cubs re-signed me. Finally, bowing to the pressure of the Chicago sports media and the Cub fans, Himes did come through with a contract offer, but it was just as insulting as the one he had made to me back before spring training.

True to form, Himes declared the contract the club's final offer and gave us a non-negotiable deadline by which we had to decide whether to accept the deal or not.

I had two choices. Number one, I could submit to Himes, who really didn't want me as part of his ball club, and suffer under his unjust ways for another year or two. Or second, I could get away from him as fast as I could.

In the most difficult decision of my life, I chose the latter. The day after I had informed him of my decision, Himes held a press conference to inform the press that I would no longer be a Chicago Cub.

Thank God that whenever the Lord closes a door, he always opens a window.

The evening following Himes's press conference to announce that I wouldn't be rejoining the Cubs, Dick called to tell me that the Boston Red Sox were very interested in making me a contract offer. What the Red Sox offered was everything and more than what I felt I deserved from the Cubs. Their offer also constituted the first time in my big-league career that a club had actually come after me.

Who knows? I thought. *Maybe it's God's will that I'm no longer a Cub. Maybe he has a purpose for me in Boston.*

With that in mind, on December 9, 1992, I officially became a member of the Boston Red Sox.

No matter how much money the Red Sox were paying me, I was still distraught over being forced to leave the Cubs. However, after a few weeks I got to know the guys on the club and began to get excited about playing my first year in Boston.

As a team, our big concern was whether we were going to be able to shake off the effects of the club's last-place finish from the year before. To enable the club to do just that was one of the primary reasons I had been signed.

During the off-season, the club had signed a few other upbeat players like me. As a result, we were playing well coming out of spring training. I hit the 400th homer of my career early in the season before hurting my knee and having to go on the disabled list. When I rejoined the club, our manager, Butch Hobson, decided to give me a shot as the team's designated hitter.

When I rejoined the team in late May, the team was on a hot streak, winning twenty-three of their last twenty-nine games and picking up a dozen games in the standings to move into first place.

From that point forward, I played almost exclusively as a DH until September 7, when the Chicago White Sox's Tim Belcher hit me with a pitch. That was the thirteenth time I was hit by a pitch that year, a career high for me. The pitch also broke a bone in my wrist.

Because of all the injuries we suffered as a team, we ended up falling out of the pennant race. Yet 1993 brought many good things along with it. The best part of the year being that I got my first opportunity to try DHing. I didn't like it very much at first, but by the end of the season I enjoyed my new role.

Andre Dawson

17

The Best Gift

In between the 1993 and '94 seasons, I took Darius and Amber over to the cemetery to visit Mamma's grave. The trip to the cemetery was the first for the both of them. Neither of them had known Mamma. Lord knows though, I wish they had.

As I stood above her grave, I began to wonder why the Lord took her before she had the opportunity to meet my children.

As I stood there with the tiny hands of both of my children in mine, the words of one of Mamma's favorite lessons came back to me.

"Pudgy," I could hear her say, "everything happens for a reason. Any time you begin to lose faith, just remember that God has a purpose for everything. Even the hairs on your head are numbered."

As I stood there, I pondered what she had told me.

I thought of my father-in-law. Only a few months before, my sister had called us. "You've got to get to South Miami," she said. "Mr. Mose is on the floor, and we can't wake him."

By the time we arrived, the paramedics were already working on my father in-law. After about fifteen minutes of trying to bring him back to life, they finally gave up and took him away in the ambulance.

Darius had been standing at my side the entire time.

Though Vanessa and I felt that both he and Amber were too young to attend his funeral, that didn't keep Darius from asking question after question about where his grandfather had gone.

Initially we hoped that he would just stop asking questions. But he didn't. So Vanessa and I decided to tell Darius that his granddad had died. That was not enough of an explanation.

"Why isn't he coming back?" he asked.

Andre Dawson

"Because he's up in heaven with God," I replied.

"What's heaven?" he asked.

"It's where God lives," Vanessa answered.

"You mean Granddad is in heaven?"

"Yes," I said.

"Where is heaven?"

"Up there," Vanessa answered, pointing to the sky as a plane passed overhead.

We had hoped that our discussion with Darius that day had satisfied his curiosity. But as we were about to find out, it only sparked further confusion.

"Darius, what's wrong?" I asked a few days later as we drove down the road and he began to cry.

"It's Granddad," he replied tearfully. "I don't want him to fall out of the plane."

"The plane?" I said. Then I realized that he must have thought that Vanessa was pointing to the plane that passed above us when she was trying to tell Darius where heaven was.

I began to smile as I thought about that conversation.

"What are you smiling at, Daddy?" he asked.

"I'm just happy to be here with the both of you," I said. Then I pointed down at the headstone. "Do you know what this is?

Both children shook their heads.

"This is the headstone of your great-grand-mother. Though she never met either of you, she would have been very proud of me for having you, more proud of me than for any game I ever played in. She was a very special person."

"Why, Daddy?" Darius asked.

"Why what, Darius?" I replied.

"Why was she such a special person?"

I didn't have to think for very long before replying. The answer came to me almost immediately.

"Because she led me to the Lord, Son. And that's the best gift anyone can ever give you."

Andre Dawson

18

A Whole New Future

I entered the '94 season with my knees feeling the best they had felt in years. As a result, I strongly leaned toward playing at least another year, if not two. I felt that 3000 hits and 500 home runs were definitely within my reach.

Then, in early May, while taking on the Cleveland Indians at Fenway Park, I hit a sharp grounder to third base and took off for first, trying to beat it out for a hit. About three-fourths of the way down the baseline, my entire left leg grabbed and became stiff. I pulled up lame as I crossed the bag, hobbled back over in the direction of my teammates, and eased myself down onto the top step of the dugout.

I sat there in pain for a few minutes. When I tried to get up, the leg stiffened even more. Each time I put weight on it, sharp pains shot up my leg and throughout my entire body. When I finally reached the trainer, I asked him to call the team doctor.

Dr. Pappas, an international authority on sports-related injuries, gave my knee a thorough examination. The next morning, he called to tell me he needed to repair the torn cartilage in my knee. Two days later I was wheeled into surgery.

I wanted desperately to start playing again as soon as possible. Within two weeks, I was in my regular spot in the line-up.

Though I experienced some discomfort as I jogged before each game, I found that I could usually massage out the tension around the knee. But that didn't last. Before long, I found it nearly impossible to run. However, since there was no swelling around the knee, I decided to hang in there.

With the Red Sox doing so well, I didn't want to quit my role as designated hitter. But with my knee acting up, it was becoming more and more possible that I might have to stick with my original plan of playing until I was forty, in which case the '94 season would be my last. If that's the way it had to be, in no way did I want to go out limping and grimacing. Like most big leaguers, I wanted to go out with a bang—with a career year or a championship ring. So I kept forcing my body back out onto the field each day.

Then, on my fortieth birthday, my knee locked up again. This time it was worse. Our trainer gave me a shot of cortisone in the knee and told me to take a few days off.

After coming back, I felt gimpy and weak-legged. It locked up again during our final July game against the A's in Oakland. In Anaheim, the next stop on our West Coast swing, I asked for and got another cortisone shot—my second in less than ten days.

While there, I decided to have the knee checked out by a Dr. Yocum, who gave me a thorough examination. Then he sat down to give me the news. My time was up. With my knees as bad as they were, playing was no longer an option, unless I wanted to risk the quality of my post-baseball life.

When we returned from the West Coast, my knee locked up on me again—this time in the middle of the night. I was put on the DL for the second time that season. This gave me an opportunity to take a good, hard look at my life.

Like every kid who has ever dreamt of being a big leaguer, I wanted to play on a World Series winning team. Naturally, I wanted my final season to end with a bang. However, in my own selfish way, I had forgotten how truly blessed I had been in my career. The Lord had carried me through one difficult experience after another. He had made me a hero in the eyes of baseball fans everywhere, and most importantly, in the eyes of my son. He had given me the opportunity to play until my fortieth birthday, which had been a goal of mine ever since I had made it to the big leagues.

But I had gotten greedy. Because the Lord had blessed me with good physical health at the beginning of the '94 season, I started dreaming of the World Series ring, the 3000 hits, and the 500 home runs. But God sent me the pain in my knee to tell me, "Enough is enough. It's time for you to retire."

I can walk away from baseball now knowing that the Lord has something planned for me beyond the game. What is that? I don't know. But I am willing to wait and listen until God reveals it to me.

My advice to any of you who read this book

Andre Dawson

is to go when the Lord calls, wherever and whenever he calls. Go whether you understand why he is calling or not. Just go. For each one of us is important to him, and each one of us has a purpose that only he knows.

For all the blessings in my life, I have no one to thank but the Lord. I'm grateful to Mamma for leading me to him. And I'm waiting eagerly for the Lord to show me my next step.